THE LITTLE BOOK OF
MOTHER'S LOVE

First published in 2025 by OH
An Imprint of HEADLINE PUBLISHING GROUP

1

Disclaimer:

Cataloguing in Publication Data is available from the British Library

ISBN 978-1-03541-984-5

Compiled and written by: Victoria Denne
Editorial: Saneaah Muhammad
Designed and typeset in Joanna Nova by: Tony Seddon
Project manager: Russell Porter
Production: Arlene Lestrade
Printed and bound in China

Headline's policy is to use papers that are natural,
renewable and recyclable products and made from wood
grown in well-managed forests and other controlled
sources. The logging and manufacturing processes are
expected to conform to the environmental regulations of
the country of origin.

HEADLINE PUBLISHING GROUP LIMITED
An Hachette UK Company
Carmelite House, 50 Victoria Embankment, London EC4Y 0DZ

The authorised representative in the EEA is Hachette Ireland, 8 Castlecourt Centre,
Castleknock Road, Castleknock, Dublin 15, D15 YF6A, Ireland

www.headline.co.uk   www.hachette.co.uk

THE LITTLE BOOK OF
MOTHER'S LOVE

THE MOST POWERFUL FORCE
ON EARTH

CONTENTS

INTRODUCTION

A mother's love is like no other – both fierce and quiet, strong and gentle, demanding and selfless, incredibly complicated and, somehow, the most simple thing on earth. It changes form and takes a new shape as her children grow and take their own steps into the world, and yet through all these variables it is always… *there*. Unrelenting and eternal. They say you only get 18 summers with your children, but being a mother is a job for life, and even when they're all grown up, they'll always be her babies.

Just as a lioness will fight to the death to protect her cubs, or an elephant will risk drowning to save her calf from a rushing river, a mother's desire to protect her children is primal, hard-wired into her from the moment she becomes one. Although, as any 14-year-old who's ever been forced to wear a sweater because their mother felt cold knows, that same protective instinct can seem a little too much at times. In truth, however, we know we'd be nowhere without them, and their love is the safe haven we return to no matter how old we get.

This little book delves into the unique characteristics of a mother's love, as well as the funny ways she has of showing it. These pages of wisdom and humour shed some light on what makes the relationship between a mother and her son so unique, before looking at the different, but no less special, bond that a mother shares with her daughter. Full of inspiring words and poignant observations from sons and daughters across the centuries and around the globe, this little book is a celebration of a love that is both deep and unswerving, limitless and ever-present, maddening (in the best way) and, above all, necessary.

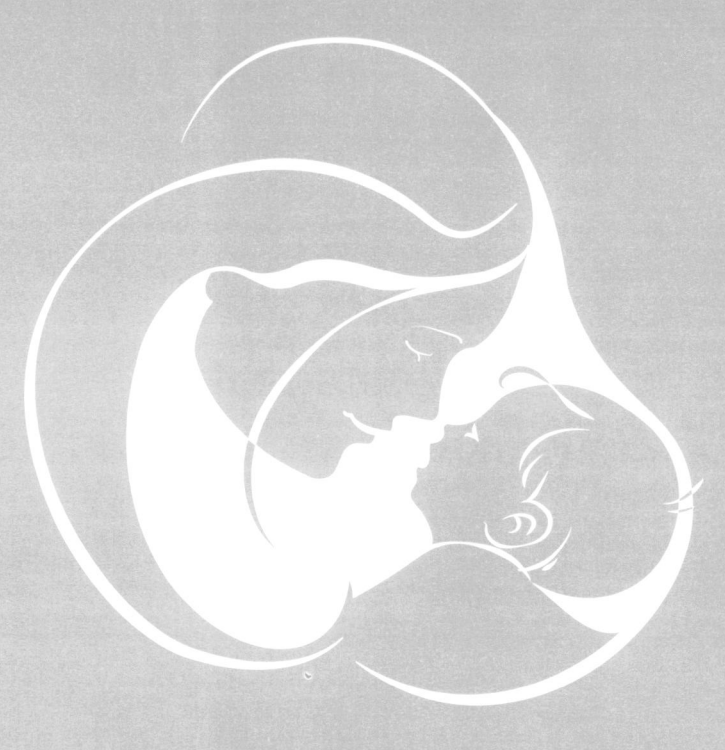

CHAPTER ONE

Mother's Intuition

First things first,
we get right to the heart of
what makes the love
that mothers have for their
children so special
and unlike any other force
on the planet.

66

When you are looking
at your mother, you are
looking at the purest
love you will ever know.

99

Charley Benetto

> **"**
> No language can
> express the power and
> beauty and heroism
> of a mother's love.
> **,,**

Edwin Hubbel Chapin

66

Mother's love is peace. It need not be acquired, it need not be deserved.

99

Erich Fromm

"

Whatever else is
unsure in this stinking
dunghill of a world a
mother's love is not.

"

James Joyce
A Portrait of the Artist as a Young Man (1916)

"

A mother's love liberates.

"

Maya Angelou

"

A mother's love for her child is like nothing else in the world. It knows no law, no pity. It dares all things and crushes down remorselessly all that stands in its path.

"

Agatha Christie
The Hound of Death and Other Stories (1933)

66

Gilbert put his arm about
them. 'Oh, you mothers!' he
said. 'You mothers! God knew
what He was about when
He made you.

99

L. M. Montgomery
Anne's House of Dreams (1917)

66

When you look into your
mother's eyes, you know that
is the purest love you can
find on this Earth.

99

Mitch Albom
For One More Day (2006)

"

The love of a mother is the
veil of a softer light between the
heart and the heavenly Father.

"

Samuel Taylor Coleridge

"

The best part of being a mom
to me is the unconditional love.
I have never felt a love as pure,
a love that's as rewarding.

"

Monica Denise Brown

66

Mother's love grows by giving.

99

Charles Lamb

66

A mother's love is patient
and forgiving when all others
are forsaking, it never fails
or falters, even though the
heart is breaking.

99

Helen Rice

"

He didn't realise that
love as powerful as your
mother's for you leaves
its own mark.

"

J. K. Rowling
Harry Potter and the Philosopher's Stone (1997)

66

There is nothing
as sincere as a
mother's kiss.

99

Saleem Sharma

"

A mother's love is more beautiful than any fresh flower.

"

Debasish Mridha

66

In the mother's eyes, her
smile, her stroking touch,
the child reads the message:
'You are there!'

99

Adrienne Rich

"

There is no velvet so soft
as a mother's lap, no rose as
lovely as her smile, no path
so flowery as that imprinted
with her footsteps.

"

Archibald Thompson

"

The clocks were striking midnight and the rooms were very still as a figure glided quietly from bed to bed, smoothing a coverlid here, settling a pillow there, and pausing to look long and tenderly at each unconscious face, to kiss each with lips that mutely blessed, and to pray the fervent prayers which only mothers utter.

"

Louisa May Alcott
Little Women (1869)

❝

Mother is the
heartbeat in the
home; and without
her, there seems to
be no heartthrob.

❞

Leroy Brownlow

66

It is the custom of every
good mother after her children
are asleep to rummage in their
minds and put things straight
for next morning, repacking
into their proper places
the many articles that have
wandered during the day.

99

J. M. Barrie
Peter Pan (1904)

66

The influence of a mother in the lives of her children is beyond calculation.

99

James E. Faust

“

Youth fades; love droops;
the leaves of friendship
fall; A mother's secret
hope outlives them all.

”

Oliver Wendell Holmes

66

Although the bond between
a mother and her child is
invisible, it's stronger than
any man-made material
in existence.

99

Ivana Davies

66

A mother would have been
always present. A mother would
have been a constant friend;
her influence would have
been beyond all other.

99

Jane Austen
Northanger Abbey (1817)

66

A mother is your first friend, your best friend, your forever friend.

99

Unknown

"

Because even if the whole world was throwing rocks at you, if you had your mother at your back, you'd be okay. Some deep-rooted part of you would know you were loved. That you deserved to be loved.

"

Jojo Moyes
One Plus One (2014)

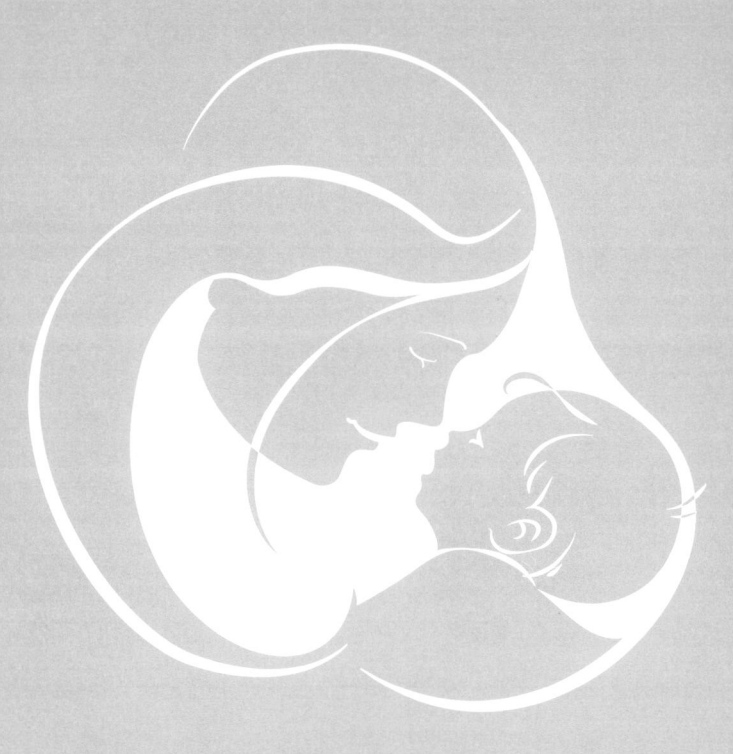

CHAPTER 2

Oh, Mother...

There is seemingly
no end to all the funny
and mildly infuriating things
mothers do for (and to!)
their children,
because — you know — they care!

66

A mom forgives us all our faults, not to mention one or two we don't even have.

99

Robert Breault

66

Sweater, n.
Garment worn by
child when its mother
is feeling chilly.

99

Ambrose Bierce

“

When your mother asks,
'Do you want a piece of advice?'
it's a mere formality. It doesn't
matter if you answer yes or no.
You're going to get it anyway.

”

Erma Bombeck

66

In the end, mothers are always right. No one else tells the truth.

99

Randy Susan Meyers

66

A mother is a person who, seeing there are only four pieces of pie for five people, promptly announces she never did care for pie.

99

Tenneva Jordan

66

God could not
be everywhere, and
therefore he made
mothers.

99

Rudyard Kipling

"

If at first you don't succeed, try doing it the way your mom told you to do it from the start.

"

Unknown

66

There are no rules in
this house. I'm not like
a regular mom, I'm a
cool mom.

99

Mrs George
Mean Girls (2004)

"

It's a funny thing about mothers... even when their own child is the most disgusting little blister you could ever imagine, they still think that he or she is wonderful.

"

Roald Dahl
Matilda (1988)

66

The first lesson every child of Athena learned: Mom was the best at everything, and you should never, *ever* suggest otherwise.

99

Rick Riordan
The Mark of Athena (2012)

"

Mom, I love you, even though I'll never accept your friend request.

"

Unknown

66

My mother's menu
consisted of two choices:
Take it or leave it.

99

Buddy Hackett

"

Nothing is really lost until your mother can't find it.

"

Unknown

66

Honey, I'm your mother. It's my job to strong-arm people into seeing how amazing you are.

99

Beverly Goldberg
The Goldbergs (2013–2023)

The best way to keep children at home is to make the home atmosphere pleasant, and let the air out of the tires.

Dorothy Parker

66

I let my kids follow their dreams, unless I already paid the registration fee on their last dream, then they follow that for 6–8 more weeks.

99

Unknown

66

A mother understands what a child does not say.

99

Jewish proverb

66

'You must never contradict
your mother,' said Miss
Serendip. 'Every mother loves
her children, and knows
what is best for them.'

99

Eric Linklater
The Wind on the Moon (1944)

66

Most mothers are instinctive philosophers.

99

Harriet Beecher Stowe

"

The most remarkable thing about my mother is that for thirty years she served the family nothing but leftovers. The original meal has never been found.

"

Calvin Trillin

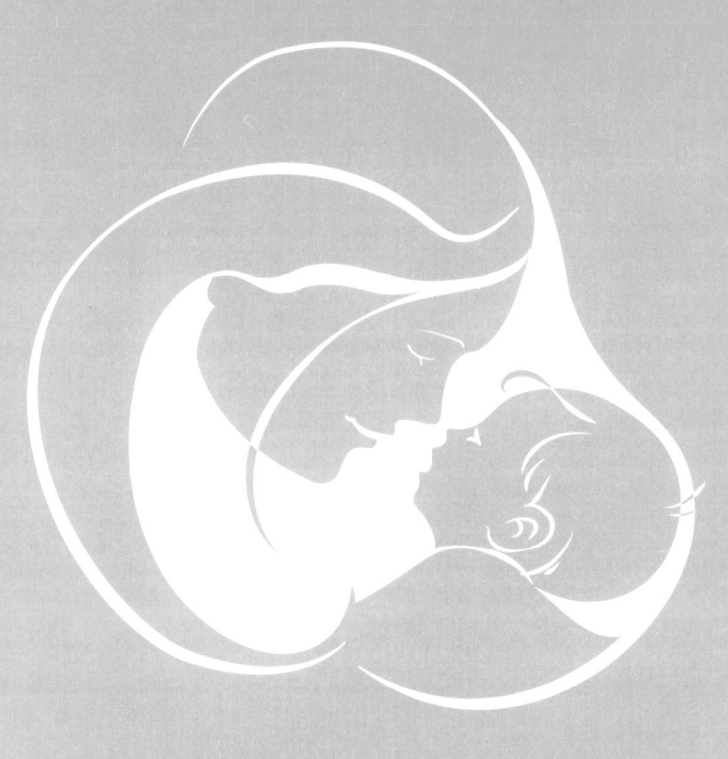

CHAPTER 3

Mothers and Sons

The love a boy feels for his mother and their bond is a defining feeling in a man's life.

Here, we dive deeper into the unique connection between mothers and their sons.

"

Maternal love is perhaps the most powerful, positive influence on a son's development and life.

"

Cheri Fuller

66

'You must feel an almost pathological need – understandably – to stand guard between your son and the world.'

'Yeah, it's called being a mother.'

99

Emma Donoghue
Room (2010)

66

My mother is my root, my foundation. She planted the seed that I base my life on, and that is the belief that the ability to achieve starts in your mind.

99

Michael Jordan

66

Moms are as relentless
as the tides. They don't
just drive us to practice,
they drive us to
greatness.

99

Steve Rushin

"

Raising boys has made me a more generous woman than I really am. Undoubtedly, there are other routes to learning the wishes and dreams of the presumably opposite sex, but I know of none more direct, or more highly motivating, than being the mother of sons.

"

Mary Blakely

66

Sons are the anchors
of a mother's life.

99

Sophocles

66

I remember my mother's prayers and they have always followed me. They have clung to me all my life.

Abraham Lincoln

66

A mother's love doesn't make her
son more dependent and timid;
it actually makes him stronger
and more independent.

99

Cheri Fuller

66

My mother had a great deal of trouble with me, but I think she enjoyed it.

99

Mark Twain

66

There is an endearing
tenderness in the love
of a mother to a son
that transcends all other
affections of the heart.

99

Washington Irving

66

Happy is the son whose faith in his mother remains unchallenged.

99

Louisa May Alcott

> **The only man who has stolen my heart is my son.**

Sandra Bullock

66

I wouldn't be doing any of this if it weren't for her, both my parents. She supported this little kid who said, 'I want to be an actor,' at 12 years old, which is ridiculous, and she drove me to all these auditions. She's the only reason I'm able to do what I do.

99

Leonardo DiCaprio

Life began with waking up and loving my mother's face.

George Eliot

66

Men are what their mothers made them.

99

Ralph Waldo Emerson

❝

A mother is the truest friend we have,
when trials, heavy and sudden, fall
upon us; when adversity takes the place
of prosperity; when friends desert
us when troubles thicken around us,
still will she cling to us, and endeavor
by her kind precepts and counsels to
dissipate the clouds of darkness, and
cause peace to return to our hearts.

❞

Washington Irving

"

The best love in the world is the love of a man. The love of a man who came from your womb, the love of your son!

"

C. JoyBell C.

66

Ain't a woman alive
who could take my
mama's place.

99

Tupac Shakur

“

My mother never gave up on me.
I messed up in school so much
they were sending me home, but
my mother sent me right back.

”

Denzel Washington

“

Even more than the time
when she gave birth, a mother
feels her greatest joy when she
hears others refer to her son
as a wise learned one.

”

Thiruvalluvar

"

My mother said to me, 'If you
are a soldier, you will become
a general. If you are a monk,
you will become the Pope.'
Instead, I became a painter,
and wound up as Picasso.

"

Pablo Picasso

> **A man loves his sweetheart the most, his wife the best, but his mother the longest.**

Irish proverb

"

Because I feel that, in the Heavens above,

The angels, whispering one to another,

Can find, among their burning
terms of love,

None so devotional as that of 'Mother',

Therefore, by that dear name
I have long called you –

You who are more than mother
unto me.

"

Edgar Allan Poe
To My Mother (1849)

66

When a man who is drinking neat gin starts talking about his mother he is past all argument.

99

C. S. Forester
The African Queen (1935)

"

You are loved for the boy you are, the man you will become, and the precious son you will always be.

"

Unknown

66

If a man has been his mother's
undisputed darling, he retains
throughout life the triumphant
feeling, the confidence in success,
which not seldom brings actual
success along with it.

99

Sigmund Freud

"

If love is as sweet
as a flower, then my
mother is that sweet
flower of love.

"

Stevie Wonder

66

They used to say, 'Oh, he's just his mother's son,' as a way of dismissing me. And every time I'd say, 'Oh, yes, thank you! I'm so proud of that.'

99

Justin Trudeau

"

Mothers are inscrutable beings to their sons, always.

"

A. E. Coppard

66

My mother was the most
beautiful woman I ever saw.
All I am, I owe to my mother.
I attribute my success in life
to the moral, intellectual
and physical education
I received from her.

99

George Washington

66

Every mother hopes that
her daughter will marry a
better man than she did and
is convinced that her son
will never find a wife as
good as his father did.

99

Martin Andersen-Nexø

66

To be a mother of a son is one
of the most important things
you can do to change the world.
Raise them to respect women,
raise them to stand up for
others, raise them to be kind.

99

Shannon L. Alder

CHAPTER 4

Mother Knows Best

Here we present a selection of classic "mother-isms" — those things only a mother would say.

Why?

Because I said so, of course!

"

'It's 'pardon',
not 'what'.

,,

"

Don't talk with
your mouth full.

"

"

Do as I say,
not as I do.

"

66

Don't make me get up and come over there!

99

66

Because I said so.

99

"

Don't sit too close
to the TV. You'll
get square eyes.

"

If someone asked you to jump off a cliff, would you?

66

Who's 'she'? The cat's mother?

99

66

As long as you live under my roof, you'll live by my rules.

99

66

Careful, the wind
will change and
your face'll stay
like that.

99

> **"**
>
> I'm not going to ask
> you again. I'm going
> to give you until the
> count of three…

... four... five... six...

99

66

I don't care who started it.

99

66

If you don't have anything nice to say, don't say anything at all.

99

66

Call me when you get there, so I know you got there safely.

99

66
Don't even
think about it…
99

"

Ask a stupid question, get a stupid answer.

"

66

I mean it: I'll stop
this car and you
can walk home.

99

" I want never gets. **"**

66

Be quiet! I can't hear myself think!

99

" Do you think I like the sound of my own voice? "

66

Eat your carrots.
They'll make you
see in the dark.

99

66

Money doesn't grow on trees, you know.

99

> **"**
> You're not going out
> looking like that.
> **"**

"

What did your last slave die of?

"

66

This is going to end in tears…

99

66

Ask your father.

99

66

I'm not asking you, I'm telling you.

99

66

Eat your dinner. There are children starving around the world.

99

66

Sarcasm is the lowest form of wit.

99

66

Don't say I didn't warn you...

99

66

If you want to
act like a child,
I'll treat you
like a child.

99

66
Just you wait until your father gets home…
99

"

Shut that door!
Were you born
in a barn?

"

"

One day, when you have children, you'll understand.

"

66

If you're too full to
finish your dinner,
then you're too full
for dessert.

99

"

Just you wait and see.

"

66
I told you so.
99

"

Don't put that in your mouth, you don't know where it's been.

"

66

You'll live.

99

CHAPTER 5

Mothers and Daughters

Along with being a parent,
mothering daughters
also means being a role model,
teaching them by example
how to be a woman and,
of course, having a best friend
for life.

66

A mother's and daughter's love is never separated.

99

Viola Shipman

66

No matter how old she may be, sometimes a girl just needs her mom.

99

Gaspard Mermillod

66

My daughter introduced me to myself… the connection I had with her when I was giving birth was something that I've never felt before.

99

Beyoncé

66

Mothers of daughters are
daughters of mothers and have
remained so, in circles joined to
circles, since time began.

99

Signe Hammer

"

When we weren't scratching
each other's eyes out, we were
making each other laugh harder
than anyone else could.

"

Lucie Arnaz

> **"**
>
> A son is a son until
> he takes him a wife,
> a daughter is a daughter
> all of her life.
>
> **"**

Irish proverb

"

To describe my
mother would be to
write about a hurricane
in its perfect power.

"

Maya Angelou

"

Mothers and daughters together are a powerful force to be reckoned with.

"

Melia Keeton-Digby

66

I'll tend her as no mother ever tended a child, a daughter.

99

Toni Morrison
Beloved (1987)

66

Mother–daughter disagreements were, in hindsight, basically mother stating the truth and daughter taking her own sweet time coming around.

99

Barbara Delinsky

"

No daughter and mother ever live apart, no matter what the distance between them.

"

Christie Watson

66

My mother… she is beautiful, softened at the edges and tempered with a spine of steel. I want to grow old and be like her.

99

Jodi Picoult

66

My mother was my role model before I even knew what that word was.

99

Lisa Leslie

"

By the time you realize
your mother was right, you
have a daughter who thinks
that you're wrong.

"

Sada Malhotra

66

My mother taught me that
there are more valuable
ways to achieve beauty than
just through your external
features. She was focused on
compassion and respect, and
those are the things that ended
up translating to me as beauty.

99

Lupita Nyong'o

> **66**
>
> As mothers and daughters, we are connected with one another. My mother is the bones of my spine, keeping me straight and true. She is my blood, making sure it runs rich and strong. She is the beating of my heart. I cannot now imagine a life without her.
>
> **99**

Kristin Hannah
Summer Island (2001)

""

Our daughters are the most precious of our treasures, the dearest possessions of our homes and the objects of our most watchful love.

""

Margaret E. Sangster

66

The relationship between
parents and children,
but especially between
mothers and daughters, is
tremendously powerful,
scarcely to be comprehended
in any rational way.

99

Joyce Carol Oates

66
What the daughter does, the mother did.
99

Jewish proverb

> **"**
> All women become like
> their mothers. That is
> their tragedy. No man
> does. That's his.
> **"**

Oscar Wilde
The Importance of Being Earnest (1895)

66

Words are not enough to
express the unconditional love
that exists between a mother
and a daughter.

99

Caitlin Houston

> **"** A mother's treasure
> is her daughter. **"**

Catherine Pulsifer

“

My mother never gave me any idea that I couldn't do whatever I wanted to do or be whomever I wanted to be… I don't know if she ever realized that the person I most wanted to be was her.

”

Rory
Gilmore Girls (2000–2007)

"

The fact is that nothing is a sacrifice for me when it comes to [my daughter]... I want to teach her how to tie her shoes, how to read, where babies come from, and about God. Just like my mom taught me.

"

Serena Williams

66

[My mother] taught me that fear is not an option.

99

Diane Von Fürstenberg

66

The more a daughter
knows the details of
her mother's life… the
stronger the daughter.

99

Anita Diamant

"

A mother is the only person
in the world who can turn
a daughter's worries and
fears into happiness.

"

Unknown

66

There were times when,
in middle school and junior
high, I didn't have a lot of
friends. But my mom was
always my friend. Always.

99

Taylor Swift

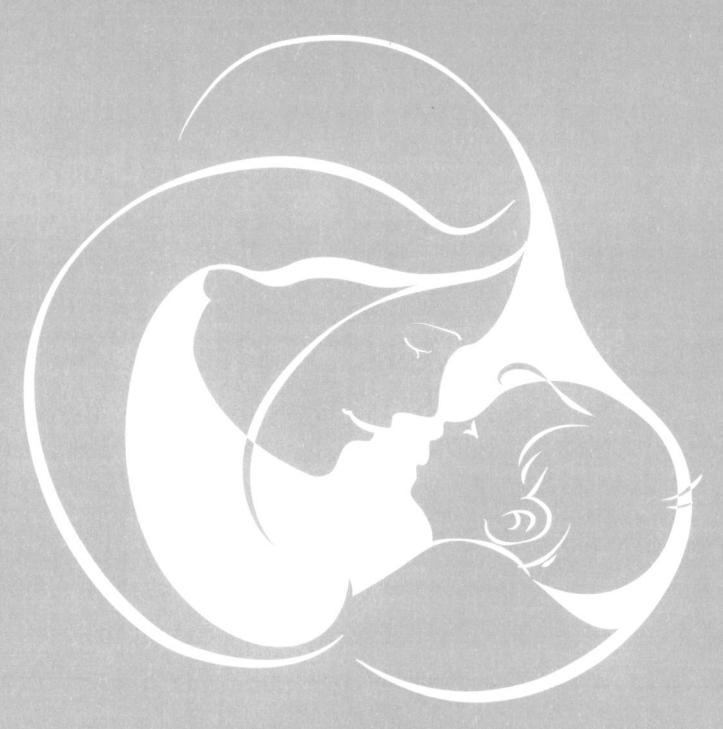

CHAPTER 6

A Mother By Any Other Name...

The love of a mother
varies across history, cultures
and from family to family,
and it reflects the beautiful
diversity of mothers themselves,
whether their children were
borne by them or not.

"

In a child's eyes, a mother is
a goddess. She can be glorious
or terrible, benevolent or filled
with wrath, but she commands
love either way. I am convinced
that this is the greatest power
in the universe.

"

N. K. Jemisin
The Hundred Thousand Kingdoms (2010)

66

A mother's happiness is like a
beacon, lighting up the future
but reflected also on the past in
the guise of fond memories.

99

Honoré de Balzac

66

Being a mother is an attitude, not a biological relation.

99

Robert A. Heinlein

66

A mother is always
the beginning. She is
how things begin.

99

Amy Tan
The Bonesetter's Daughter (2001)

66

The loveliest masterpiece of the heart of God is the heart of a mother.

99

St. Thérèse of Lisieux

66

I really saw clearly, and for the
first time, why a mother is really
important. Not just because she feeds
and also loves and cuddles and even
mollycoddles a child, but because in
an interesting and maybe an eerie and
unworldly way, she stands in the gap.
She stands between the unknown
and the known.

99

Maya Angelou
Mom & Me & Mom (2013)

"

Biology is the least of what makes someone a mother.

"

Oprah Winfrey

66

I go back to that one moment when I stood in the driveway with small rocks and clumps of dirt around my feet and looked back at the porch. And there they were. All these mothers. I have more mothers than any eight girls off the street. They are the moons shining over me.

99

Sue Monk Kidd
The Secret Life of Bees (2001)

66

We are born of love;
love is our mother.

99

Rumi

66

Not flesh of my flesh, nor
bone of my bone, but still
miraculously my own. Never
forget for a single minute,
you didn't grow under
my heart, but in it.

99

Fleur Conkling Heyliger

"

Heaven lies beneath the feet of mothers.

"

Prophet Muhammad
(peace be upon him)

66

It may be possible to
gild pure gold, but who
can make his mother
more beautiful?

99

Mahatma Gandhi

66

No mother is ever, completely,
a child's idea of what a mother
should be, and I suppose it works
the other way around as well.

99

Margaret Atwood
The Handmaid's Tale (1985)

"

Mothers and their children
are in a category all their own.
There's no bond so strong in
the entire world. No love so
instantaneous and forgiving.

"

Gail Tsukiyama
Dreaming Water (2003)

"

Mothers, I believe, intoxicate us.
We idolize them and take them for
granted. We hate them and blame
them and exalt them more thoroughly
than anyone else in our lives. We sift
through the evidence of their love,
reassure ourselves of their affection and
its biological genesis. We can steal and
lie and leave and they will love us.

"

Megan Mayhew Bergman
Birds of a Lesser Paradise (2012)

> **"**
>
> She was of the stuff of which great men's mothers are made. She was indispensable to high generation, hated at tea parties, feared in shops, and loved at crises.
>
> **"**

Thomas Hardy
Far From the Madding Crowd (1874)

"

Mothers were the only ones you could depend on to tell the whole, unvarnished truth.

"

Margaret Dilloway
How to Be an American Housewife (2010)

"

'The door,' replied Maimie,
'will always, always be open,
and mother will always be
waiting at it for me.'

"

J. M. Barrie
The Little White Bird (1902)

> **"**
>
> And all my mother
> came into mine
> eyes. And gave me
> up to tears.
>
> **"**

William Shakespeare
Henry V (1599)

66

Mother love is the
fuel that enables a
normal human being
to do the impossible.

99

Marion C. Garretty

66

Momma reminds me to breathe, the same way she did before I outgrew asthma. I think she stays in my room the whole night, 'cause every time I wake up, she's sitting on my bed.

99

Angie Thomas
The Hate U Give (2017)

66

She taught me what's
important, and what isn't.
And I've never forgotten. And
that's what mothers do, I say.

99

Steven Herrick
A Place Like This (1998)

66

A mother's hug lasts long after she lets go.

99

Unknown

66

For whom will a woman lie?
Sometimes for herself.
Usually for the man she loves.
Always for her children.

99

Agatha Christie
The Murder on the Links (1923)

66

Mother is the name for
God in the lips and hearts
of little children.

99

William Makepeace Thackeray

66

Mothers are like glue. Even
when you can't see them, they're
still holding the family together.

99

Susan Gale

66

I will look after you and I will
look after anybody you say
needs to be looked after,
any way you say. I am here.
I brought my whole self to
you. I am your mother.

99

Maya Angelou
Mom & Me & Mom (2013)